THE BALANCED LIFE:

THE PRACTICAL USE

OF THE

WHOLE ARMOR OF GOD

Allen L. Elder

Walk in the Spirit, and you will never sin.
(Galatians 5:16) AEP

This book is dedicated to my three sons;
Trey, Blake, and Scott,
mighty men of God.

TABLE OF CONTENTS

INTRODUCTION

The spiritual warfare is real. The adversary has many weapons to use against us. We can become so taken and distracted with the warfare that we are unable to give time, attention, and effort to our specific ministry for the Lord in fulfillment of his great commission. Properly wearing the whole armor of God is our defense and relief from over-preoccupation with our spiritual foes. This is not to diminish the importance of the warfare but to bring awareness to God's provision for it, and to say that when we properly wear the whole armor of God, much of the adversary's weapons and warfare against us are brought into subjection, freeing us to do God's will.

My prayer for you is that as you read this book that God, the Holy Spirit, will illuminate your heart and teach you how to wear the whole armor of God as it was intended to be worn. And, that you will put it on and leave it on for the rest of your life so you can accomplish down to the last detail the assignment God has given you.

Allen L. Elder
www.thelifenetwork.online

CHAPTER 1

THE WHOLE ARMOR OF GOD: GETTING IT RIGHT

Wherefore take unto you the whole armor of God, that ye may be able to withstand in the evil day, and having done all, to stand.
(Ephesians 6:13)

God created the earth and everything in it and called it good. We can all attest to the goodness of God's creation. We have eaten off the milk and meat of the land. We have quinched our thirst from its bubbling springs and sparkling waters. We have refreshed ourselves from the fruits of its trees and vines. We have rested and relaxed by the rolling waves of its seashores. Yes, the earth is a good place.

On the other hand, we do not have to look very far to know that something has gone awry. There is a fly in the ointment, and it's pretty obvious. We have those experiences when in spite of all we can do, nothing goes the way it should. We make our plans, and they turn out horribly. We try to do or say something nice, and it is taken the wrong way. We do our best and we are left empty-handed. For all of our best efforts at times, things turn out the opposite from what we would like them to be. Other times, we feel the oppression and whether we want to or not, we have to take up a defense

1

against an unseen adversary. What is the problem, and how do we deal with it? Is there a way to meet these inconsistencies consistently and effectively? Yes, and the way to do it is by wearing the whole armor of God.

Many a book and commentary has been written about the whole armor of God. Do we really need another one? By now, haven't we heard and learned everything there is to know about this subject? I don't think we can ever say that about anything from the Bible. If all the books were written about Jesus that ought to be written, and if the world itself can not contain them, there is obviously more than we could ever learn about him and his way of life. As the Bible says, O the depth of the riches both of the wisdom and knowledge of God! How unsearchable are his judgements, and his ways past finding out! (Romans 11:33). How can finite mankind exhaust any subject from the Word of God? So, yes, we need another book on the whole armor of God. And yes, we need this one because, I guarantee you, you have never seen this subject in the light in which you are about to see it.

I have read and heard many of the angles from which the armor has been approached. One man said every morning before he gets out of the bed, he imagines himself putting on each piece of the armor. Another one said, "When the enemy attacks, grab the armor and put it on and you'll be ready for anything the devil throws at you." These comments sound good. The problem is that in themselves, they are useless. Simply imagining a thing as magnificent as the whole armor of God or trying to put it on in a moment's notice ignores the reality and context of its power. There is a certain way to be clothed in the armor and these ways do not get the job done.

Years ago, God gave me a new angle on the whole armor of God; new in the sense that I had never heard or seen before or since. It was in the middle of July

1988, 35 years ago at the time of this writing. Our second son had just been born. I had been reading the book of Ephesians which is my favorite book of the Bible. (I usually say this no matter which book I am reading, even Leviticus). After several readings of the book, my mind was keenly attune to its content. One morning very early, around two am, I awakened to one thought which blazed across my mind like a comet in the night sky. The thought from God was this: "The whole armor of God is not some kind of magic words we say in a time of trouble; it is a lifestyle." I thought, this thought is too good for me to roll over and go back to sleep. I probably won't remember it in the morning. So, I got up from the bed, went to my desk and wrote the thought on a sheet of paper exactly as I had heard it in my spirit, and went back to bed and back to sleep.

Later in the morning when it was really time to get up, I went back to my desk and read the sentence I had written, "The whole armor of God is not some kind of magic words we say in a time of trouble; it is a lifestyle." I began to look through the book of Ephesians again, this time I could see how the book outlined around the pieces of the armor. Next, the Holy Spirit gave me some practical understanding about how each piece applies to the way we are to live this whole armor of God lifestyle. It made perfect sense to me. Since then, this is the way I have tried to live my life. It is the way I have been teaching others about how to live their life, to wear the whole armor of God, and to win the spiritual warfare.

Recently, I had the opportunity to teach on the subject with one of our small groups at our church. They were encouraged by the teaching and so was I. In fact, I was so encouraged, I decided it was time to put this down in a book. Upon this decision, it was as if I could hear the Holy Spirit say, "Well, it's about time. I gave this to you 35 years ago. You have never seen it in anyone else's book. You have never heard it this way in another person's sermon. I gave it this way to you, and I want you to be the one to write it in a book."

A couple of weeks later, I was having lunch with one of my dear friends. I told him that I was about to start a new book on the whole armor of God. He said that he loved this subject and had memorized this passage from the Word. I said, "You've never heard it the way I am about to share it with you", and he said, "Let's hear it; I'm all ears." So, I gave it to him in about 15 minutes the way the Lord gave it to me. He was truly moved by it and said, "This has to be your next book. Christians need to see the armor this way. The church needs this book."

Now, here it is. We believe we have been obedient to the heavenly calling to put this whole armor of God lifestyle in a book. After 35 years of living it, I can personally testify to the fact that it works in the way you are about to see it. Others to whom I have explained it and who have applied it in their own lives can testify to the validity of it as well. My prayer is that by the end of this book, you will be equipped with some of the most wonderful truth that you have needed to hear your entire life, and you will be on your way to becoming one of a great cloud of witnesses who can say from experience, this is the way we should walk in the salvation that Christ has given us in the world in which we live.

THERE IS A WARFARE

Even if we did not know what the Bible says about the spiritual warfare, we know there is one because we have experienced it many times in our life. Thank God, we have what the Bible says on this subject. And it's what the Bible has to say that makes all the difference in whether we win or lose the warfare. Ephesians 6:10-

12 tells us how to approach this delicate subject of the Christian life and how to be victorious in it. There are three steps to the approach.

Step one, we are to approach the spiritual warfare in the power of the Lord (v10). In ourselves, we are no match for the adversary; the devil and his demons. They are fallen angels. They are of a higher order of creation than man. They have supernatural powers and abilities which we do not have apart from God. When we face off with these spiritual enemies in our own strength, we will fail every time. Remember the seven sons of Sceva in Acts 19 who tried to do this and lost. We should not be as foolish to come against our enemy in the strength of our flesh. The flesh is weak, spiritually speaking, and again, no match for the enemy. On the other hand, our adversary is no match for the believer who is indwelt and filled with the Holy Spirt and clothed with the whole armor of God. In this light, we are more powerful than the enemy because God is at home and living in us and through us. Let this always be the first thing you do when engaging in the spiritual warfare; renounce your own strength and be strong in the Lord and in the power of his might.

Step two is given to us in the next verse, put on the whole armor of God (v11). We are commanded to put on the armor. This is a decision that we must come to at some point in our Christian experience. We must decide that we are going to be clothed continuously in the whole armor of God. Nothing else will do. We must decide to put on the armor and leave it on for as long as we live. The only way to do this is to wear it as a lifestyle. We are commanded to put on the armor but are never commanded to take it off. Hence, the reason so many Christians live defeated lives: they put on the armor and take it off in the same way that they clothe themselves each day with physical clothing.

We are to put on the whole armor of God. This is a good place to say that the armor is a package deal. Another reason for failure in the Christian life is that some Christians try to put on some of the armor but not every piece. This does not work. The armor is a unit and every piece is needed and is there for a reason. Like the members of the body of Christ, the pieces of the armor blend in with and support each other. One piece is connected to another in such a way that we need every piece. To leave a piece or some pieces off is to make vulnerable to attack certain areas of your life. To miss a single piece of the armor is to cause the whole armor to not be as effective as it could be. We need to put on every piece of the armor and leave it on. We can do this when we realize that wearing the armor is a way of life.

One of the first benefits of putting on the whole armor of God is that we will be able to stand against the wiles of the devil. The devil employs many wiles against us. He has many schemes, tricks, crafty methods, deceitful approaches, and traps to lay against us. We are at war with an enemy who has already lost the warfare and who is desperate to take down as many Christ followers as possible on his way to the lake of fire. He will stop at nothing in his attempt to steal, kill, and destroy us. We have to be on the alert. We must be sober and vigilant because he is seeking whom he may devour. Wearing the whole armor of God is our defense against these methods of attack.

Step three in the approach to the spiritual warfare is to have the proper perspective on who our enemy actually is (v12). The enemy is not the person with whom we may have a conflict, although the enemy certainly can use people against us. The real enemy is a spiritual one manifested in the person of Satan and his demonic army. Terms like principalities, powers, rulers of the darkness of this world, and spiritual wickedness in high places are rank and file of the demonic army assembled against us for spiritual combat. The enemy is not primarily flesh and blood. Fleshly weapons do not work against a spiritual foe. Realizing that the enemy is a spiritual one causes us to take up spiritual weapons and spiritual weaponry gets the job done. Our adversary knows this. We need to know it also.

It is also important that we realize that Satan himself is not our primary enemy in the daily spiritual warfare. Of course, he is behind it all, but we do not directly wrestle with him on a daily basis. He is like us in that as a created being he can only be in one place at a given time. He is not like God who is omnipresent: everywhere at the same time. Satan does not possess this attribute, hence just one of the reasons he can never be God. He does, however, have an innumerable host of demons he can send against us. It is of vital importance that we know that they, like their Commander, Satan, were defeated by Jesus Christ at the cross (Colossians 2:15). This is the ultimate reason we can win the spiritual warfare every time.

This little three-verse passage in Ephesians is packed full of good news for the believer in Christ. You would be wise to remember it and go back to it again and again. Learn the correct approach to the subject of spiritual warfare and use it. This is one of the keys to living in the victory Christ has already won on our behalf.

SOME THINGS TO KNOW ABOUT OUR ADVERSARY

Since we have an adversary, Satan, and since he is behind all the demonic activity that we encounter, it would be helpful for us to know some things about him and his accomplices. Read over the list below. Which of these were you aware of? Which facts are new to you?

These facts are basic information the Bible gives us about our spiritual enemy. Concerning our adversary, the Bible tells us:

1. We have one.
   Your adversary (1 Pet 5:8)

2. Who they are.
   A. Your adversary the devil (1 Pet 5:8)
   B. Demons (Eph 6:12)

3. They are already defeated. They were defeated by Jesus Christ at the cross.
   (Col 2:14-15)

4. They cannot do any more to us than God will allow.
   (Job 2:6)

5. They cannot do any more to us they we will allow.
   (Luke 10:17)

6. How to walk in victory over the adversary.
   A. Wear the whole armor of God (Eph 6:10-18)
   B. Use the weapons of our warfare (2 Cor 10:3-6)
   C. Give no place to the devil (Eph 4:27)
   D. Do not be ignorant of his devices (2 Cor 2:11)
   E. Stand against the wiles of the devil (Eph 6:11)
   F. Resist the devil and he will flee from you (Jas 4:7)
   G. Resist steadfast in the faith (1 Pet 5:9)

7. The adversary's goal is to destroy you.
   The thief has come to steal, kill, and to destroy (John 10:10)

8. The adversary has been working on this plan from before you were born.

(He copies God's strategies and modes of operation)

9. You can neutralize much of the adversary's activity and success in your life by learning and living the whole armor of God lifestyle.

HERE'S THE LAYOUT

Before we can live the whole armor of God lifestyle, we need to know what the whole armor of God actually is. This is one of those places where many of the teachers and commentators disagree. I have seen listed as few as five pieces of the armor and as many as eight or nine pieces. What is the correct number of pieces of the armor? The Bible names seven pieces in Ephesians 6:13-18. Let's name them now.

1. The Girdle of Truth
2. The Breastplate of Righteousness
3. The Shoes of the Preparation of the Gospel of Peace
4. The Shield of Faith
5. The Helmet of Salvation
6. The Sword of the Spirit
7. Prayer

Getting the number correct is critical to our success in this lifestyle. Missing a piece or pieces can harm us, as we have stated previously. Adding pieces brings harm to that which God has already perfected and provided. Having seven pieces, we can see that there is a center point, or balance point in the armor lifestyle. The center point is the shield of faith. Now isn't this interesting? How is it that the Bible says a Christian should walk in this world? By faith, right? So, the middle or balance point in the lifestyle is that we walk by faith, being protected as if by a shield.

Since the shield of faith is the balance point, we also observe that three pieces of the armor come before the shield of faith, and three pieces come after the shield of faith. From this configuration we can see that the first three pieces help us to begin to walk by faith, and the last three pieces help us to continue to walk by faith.

Look at Figure 1-1 in Appendix 1. This is a simple balance beam. It shows a beam sitting upon a balance point like the seesaw we used to play on as children. Note the three pieces on the left side; the first three pieces of the whole armor of God. Note also the last three pieces of the whole armor of God on the right side of the beam. And note the shield of faith in the center. This is what a balanced life of walking by faith looks like. When the armor is in the proper place, we can have balance, and we can walk by faith.

Now that we know the number of pieces of the armor and what they are called, let's make a practical application of each one of them. The practical application is a phrase which tells us of one of the seven aspects of a balanced walk of faith. Let's list them below.

1. The Girdle of Truth = Correct Doctrine
2. The Breastplate of Righteousness = Comprehending Correct Doctrine
3. The Shoes of the Preparation of the Gospel of Peace = Carrying Out Correct Doctrine
4. The Shield of Faith = The Consistent Walk of Faith
5. The Helmet of Salvation = The Clean Mind
6. The Sword of the Spirit = Combatting the Enemy
7. Prayer = Communion with God

Knowing the correct number of pieces of the whole armor of God and the practical application of each piece is key to wearing the armor as a lifestyle and to winning the daily spiritual warfare.

THE PRACTICAL USE OF THE WHOLE ARMOR OF GOD

Now, let's walk through how this armor is a lifestyle, or a way of life, how it works in a practical way, protecting us in the spiritual warfare. When we read the Bible, God shows us his truth. Truth is the immovable foundation that we stand upon in the Christian life. It is the truth that gives us a firm foundation of strength on which and from which to live our life in Christ. But just to know the truth is not enough. Truth has to develop into understanding. We have to comprehend the truth that we know in order for it to do us any good. When we understand the truth, we have to take it a step farther and begin to apply this truth in our life. We have to start walking out the truth that God gives us. We have to obey the Word. We have to adjust and arrange our life according to the Word and ways of God. This is the process we go through which gets us started in walking by faith. When we have done this enough times, we begin to be consistent at it and before long we can see that we are walking by faith.

If we are to continue to walk by faith, we will have to keep our mind clean. This is where the helmet of salvation comes in. We have to get our thinking right. We have to arrest and control every thought that comes across our mind. We have to learn to think on things that are pure and righteous, and holy, not allowing our minds to be carried away and held captive by hellish and impure thinking. This process will not come easy. We will find that this is where we will engage the enemy in spiritual hand to hand combat with the sword of the Spirit, which is the Word of God. This does not mean that the enemy puts up less of a fight when it comes to knowing, comprehending, or applying truth in your life. These are areas where his attacks are not so apparent. He is subtle, and he can hide very well in these areas,

11

ever so slightly twisting truth to the point where it is difficult to detect. But with our thoughts and in our minds, this is as raw as it gets. The enemy pushes the outside of the envelope here. If they can win the battle of our thoughts, they can control us by oppression. Sometimes in this part of the warfare, we might even fight to a standstill, but we can win if we stand and having done all to stand. In the midst of it all, we can have sweet communion with God through the sword of the Spirit, God's Word, and through prayer. In the Word, he speaks to us and guides us in our praying. In prayer we speak to him and he also speaks to us. It is in these times of communion with God that he heals us from the wounds we encounter in the spiritual combat, and gives us confidence to walk with him, standing against our adversary.

That was one cycle through the armor. When we commune with God through his Word and prayer, God shows us more truth. We have to do the work we need to do that we might understand the new truth he has shown us. We have to apply it to our life; to incorporate it into the way we live our life for God on God's terms. As we walk it out, we find that we are getting more consistent in the areas where God has shown us more truth. The truth is making us free. And we're free to walk with God in this world. Knowing this new truth has opened up more areas in which we have to fight to keep our mind and thinking free. Our adversary will not take our progress lying down. They will work to rob it from us. Again, we will have to fight, standing upon the Word of God. After the battle, we can have more communion with God through his Word and through prayer. When this happens, God will again show us more truth, and the cycle starts over again. This is a continual process which produces an encircling of the armor about us, a shield of faith and protection which deflects all of the fiery darts of the enemy. It works a little like the atmosphere around planet earth, deflecting objects in space from ever reaching the earth and doing their damage.

This is the way of life we need to live as Christians, truly wearing the whole armor of God. Can you see by this explanation why it is useless to imagine putting on the armor as opposed to living in this way? Can you see that it is useless to try to grab the armor when we realize we are under spiritual attack, like we would grab an umbrella to protect us from a sudden summer shower of rain? The armor lifestyle is an ongoing exercise in understanding the truth of God's Word to the point of obeying and living it consistently, beating down the enemy when they try to make us do otherwise, and searching the Word of God for more truth to understand and obey. Imagining and trying to grab the armor when we need it leaves us defeated, wondering why the armor did us no good when we needed it the most. This whole armor of God lifestyle which could be summarized simply as walking in the Word, or walking in the Spirit, actually produces the results we need and want, helping us live a life that pleases God, is victorious for us, and leaves Satan and his demons with more losses in the spiritual warfare.

Now that we have explained the whole armor of God lifestyle, take a good look at Figure 1-2 in Appendix 1. This figure shows the cycle we have just given, starting from the top of the circle and traveling around the sphere in a clockwise direction. Note that when it has made a complete loop that it starts over again and continues in this way. On the outside layer we see the names of the seven pieces of the whole armor of God as the Bible states them. Underneath these names are the portions of Paul's letter to the Ephesians which correspond to each piece of the armor. The inner layer shows the practical application of the whole armor of God in our daily life. And at last, the innermost circle represents the Christian who is consistently walking by faith and who is protected as a result of the way he lives his life, walking in the Word of God. How does this explanation compare to the way you have been trying to live your life as a Christian? This way of life includes and encompasses every possible thing in the Christian life. Which way of life would produce best the results God wants us to have? Are you willing to adopt this way of life for the rest of your life on earth?

Going forward, we will look at each piece of the whole armor of God. We will see what it is to wear it and receive its benefits and blessings.

CHAPTER 2

THE GIRDLE OF TRUTH

CORRECT DOCTRINE

Stand therefore, having your loins girt about with truth
(Ephesians 6:14a)

That which we call the book of Ephesians consists of six chapters. The passage on the whole armor of God is found in the last chapter of the book. It is the key to understanding the content of this book, or letter, or epistle as it is called in the old Bibles. The whole armor of God outlines the book for us. Beginning with chapter one and continuing through the entire book and in consecutive order, we find the pieces of the whole armor of God. We find also that the armor is indeed a way of life. It is not magic words that we say hurriedly when we realize we are under the attack of the enemy. When we live the way of life of walking with God in his Word, we will find that the armor has deflected much of the enemy's attacks against us without our even being aware of it. This frees us up to give more time and energy to the work God has called us to do in the fulfilling of the great commission. The part the warfare of which we are aware can be faced more confidently and successfully as this way of life reduces

15

our adversary's arsenal against us. When we walk with the Lord in the light of his Word, as the songwriter of old wrote, we find that we are walking by faith in the way of victory.

The first half of the first chapter of Ephesians gives us the first piece of the armor, the girdle of truth (1:1-14). The girdle is like the large leather belt worn by a weightlifter. It gives him a foundation of strength for his back. We also see many people who do a lot of lifting and physical labor wearing this kind of belt or girdle. The believer in Christ is provided the girdle of truth, a foundation of our strength in Christ.

The girdle of truth is truth itself. Truth is found in the Word of God, both living and written. The living Word is Jesus who said, "I am the way, the truth, and the life" (John 14:6). The written Word is the revelation of God in the Bible. Practically speaking, we called the girdle of truth, correct doctrine. In the first half of Ephesians chapter one, we have more doctrine than the church has been able to digest or keep up with in the last 2,000 years.

Within this little section of Scripture are some of the deepest doctrinal waters found in the Bible. The first three verses are easy waters into which we can wade. But with our first step into verse four, it is as if we step into a drop-off and quickly go into these doctrinal waters over our heads. We cannot touch the bottom and we may even find ourselves strangling a bit, having taken in some of these waters into our spiritual nose, mouth, and lungs. We will have to come up for air time and time again in our attempt to get our feet established on these solid waters of truth, walking on them as it were when Jesus and Peter walked upon the waters of the Sea of Galilee.

In this section of Scripture, we find 10 doctrines that every believer should know and grasp. These truths are called spiritual blessings in heavenly places in Christ. Blessing 1 is related to the Father, Son, and Holy Spirit. Blessings 2-5 are related to the Father. Blessings 6-8 are related to the Son. And blessings 9-10 are related to the Holy Spirit. These doctrines are what some of the writers referred to as the meat of the word. Some of these doctrines will shake your faith to the core. When God shakes our faith, only the eternal things will remain. Everything else will fall away. As I introduce you to these doctrines, I ask you to study them for yourself and ask God to show them to you.

We get so taken up with what the Bible says or does not say about the antichrist, the false prophet, the two witnesses, or the 144,000, etc., and we pay little attention to what the Bible says about the child of God. Thus, we are tossed to and fro with every wind of doctrine, being deceived, doubting our salvation, and wondering if we ever do get it, will we have it forever? What is more dangerous and destructive in the life of a believer than the devil and demons is the ignorance of the child of God concerning the deep doctrines of the Word of God. Many believers have not studied these doctrines and are not settled upon them. God said, "My people are destroyed for lack of knowledge" (Hos 4:6), and "You shall know the truth and the truth shall make you free" (John 8:32).

My advice is to take these 10 doctrines and stop being distracted with controversy over them. Stop discounting and denying them as if they are not true. Study them for all they are worth. Cry over them, wrangle with them, pull your hair out over them, until you get settled upon them, like Jacob did when he wrestled with God at Peniel (Genesis 32:24-32). Get settled on them and embrace them. Stand on them as the basis of your eternal salvation, the foundation of your strength, and as your defense against an adversary who is walking about, devouring every believer who has not come to grips with these issues. Pick out the ones you are not settled on and wrestle with them until you get settled. As God gives you light into these doctrines, you will be glad he did, and you will have the most sure spiritual footing you have ever had in your life.

Now, let's name these ten doctrines which every believer should know. They are the sovereignty of God (v5,9,11); election (v4); predestination (v5,11); adoption (v5); acceptance (v6); redemption (v7); forgiveness (v7); inheritance (v11); salvation (v13); and sealing (v13). Read the list again. Just the mention of some of these doctrines may cause a bit of anxiety to well up in some of us for various reasons. We have seen brothers and sisters in Christ debate and divide over some of them. We have tried to understand them but are still left with many unanswered questions. And, we may wonder if we are even included among those to whom these spiritual blessings apply. From this point on, may I suggest to all of us that we receive these doctrines as our friends. They are given to show us what God has done in saving us, in providing the eternal security of our salvation in Christ, and for our strength as long as we live on the earth.

These doctrines have been studied, pondered, debated, dissected, written about, preached, received, resisted and rejected for centuries. My purpose here is obviously not to try to present every possible thought or statement regarding them, or even to state every detail within each one of them. Neither is my purpose to try to convince you of their truth. Only God can do this. I simply want to point them out and give you some framework on which to consider and study them for yourself, and to make your own discoveries. Following is a brief, very brief, description of the doctrines Paul includes as a part of the girdle of truth.

1. THE SOVEREIGNTY OF GOD (v5, v9, v11)

God rules over all creation. He alone is God. There

is none beside him. He does as he pleases. He is his own counsel. All creation is subject unto Him, especially man.

2. ELECTION (v4)
A. Definition: God's pretemporal choice of those who would be saved.
B. Believers are chosen by God:
   1) Before the foundation of the world (Eph 1:4)
   2) According to the foreknowledge of God (1 Pet 1:2)
   3) By the grace of God, not by human acts or works (Rom 11:5-6) (Eph 2:8-9)
C. 2 Questions
   1) Why witness if God has elected?
      a) We are not sent to make the gospel acceptable (only God can do this); we are sent to make the gospel available.
      b) God has not only ordained the end but also the means to the end. This means our witnessing is part of the process God uses to bring others to salvation.
      c) We do not know who the elect are until after they are saved, therefore we are to make the gospel available to everyone and trust God to call the elect unto salvation.
   2) How can we know we are among the elect of God?
      By our response to the gospel (Rom 10:9-10) (1 Thes 1:4-10)
      If we believe on Jesus in our heart and confess him with our mouth, we can be sure that we are among the elect of God and that we are saved.
D. This doctrine is part of the larger doctrine of the sovereignty of God. It should also be considered in light of the total depravity of man.

3. PREDESTINATION (v5,11)

A. Definition: God's pretemporal planning of the destiny of the elect.
B. Believers are predestined to:
    1) Adoption into God's family (Eph 1:5)
    2) To be conformed to the image of Christ (Rom 8:29-30)
    3) To an inheritance in Christ (Eph 1:11)
C. To refuse predestination is to refuse the purpose of God in your life (Eph 1:11)
    It is to say:
    1) I do not want to be adopted into the family of God
    2) I do not want to be conformed to the image of Christ
    3) I do not want my inheritance in Christ
D. Election looks back into eternity past, predestination looks ahead into eternity future.

4. ADOPTION (v5)

A. Definition: Placing the believer in God's family as an adult child with all the rights and privileges thereof.
B. Adoption means:
    1) Relationships to the prior family are all dissolved.
    2) We have full rights and privileges of the family of God.
    3) We have access to God and a personal relationship with him.
C. Privileges of adoption (Rom 8:14-17)
    1) Walk – Led by the Spirit
    2) Freedom – Out of bondage
    3) Talk – We cry out to God
    4) Assurance – The Spirit bears witness
    5) Inheritance – Heirs
    6) Suffering – Suffering and glory

5. ACCEPTED (v6) [Grace]
    A. Definition: God has shed his grace upon us and we are accepted into his family.
    B. Highly favored
    C. Make acceptable
    D. Made accepted

6. REDEMPTION (v7)
    A. Definition: To deliver by paying a price.
    B. The story of redemption is told in three words:
        1) To go to the market – (Rev 5:9) [agorazo]
        2) To purchase out of the market and never sell again – (Gal 3:13) [exagorazo]
        3) To set free – (Eph 1:7,14) [apolytrosis]
    C. Redemption is eternal (Heb 9:12)

7. FORGIVENESS (v7)
    A. Definition: To pardon or grant relief from payment.
    B. God did not simply excuse us or declare us not guilty but pardoned us because the full penalty of our sin was paid in full by Christ; Christ shed his blood for the remission (forgiveness) of sin (Matt 26:28) (John 19:30) (1 John 2:2)
    C. Since the price has been paid, we have been released from the penalty of sin and it will never be brought up again.

8. INHERITANCE (v11)
    A. General statements:
        1) Christ is the heir of God since he is the Son of God (Heb 1:2)
        2) Through redemption, believers are sons of God by adoption and are fellow-heirs with Christ (Rom 8:17) (Gal 4:7)
        3) The Holy Spirit is the guarantee of our inheritance (Eph 1:14)

4) Christ and his kingdom are the inheritance both in the present and in the eternal future (Matt 25:34)
B. Specific statements:
1) Our inheritance is Christ and is in Christ (Eph 1:10-11)
2) It is an eternal inheritance (Heb 9:15)
3) It is incorruptible (1 Pet 1:4)
4) It is undefiled (1 Pet 1:4)
5) It fadeth not away (1 Pet 1:4)
6) It is reserved in heaven for us (1 Pet 1:4)

9. SAVED (v13)

A. The saving work of the Holy Spirit (regeneration, the new birth) is done quietly (John 3:8). The Spirit has been there and done his work before we know it. Salvation is of the Lord (Jonah 2:9).
B. Yet (v13) says:
1) We trusted
2) We heard
3) We believed
4) These are not the causes but the consequences of salvation.
5) No one can call Jesus Lord but by the Holy Spirit (1 Cor 12:3)

10. SEALED (v13-14) (Eph 4:30) (2 Cor 2:22)

A. We are sealed by the Holy Spirit when he indwells us (Eph 4:30)
B. The seal indicates:
1) Authority
2) Ownership
3) Responsibility for
4) Endorsement
5) Security
C. The seal of the Spirit is God's guarantee that he is going to complete that which he has started in us

(Eph 1:14) (Phil 1:6)
Earnest = pledge, surety, down-payment,
guarantee.

These doctrines are given to us by God in order to show us what he has done in saving us. He has left no stone unturned and no possibility that we could ever be lost again. These doctrines are the foundation of our faith in Christ. When we begin to understand them, embrace them, and stand upon them, we find that we have a sure footing on which to walk with God, build our life and ministry, and live in victory over our adversary, the devil and demons. The devil, of course, has other plans for these doctrines. He is masterful at using the Word of God against believers, and he will certainly use these wonderful doctrines against us if he can. In the space below, we can see how he does this with each one of these doctrines which make up the girdle of truth. In the first list is the truth from God's perspective. The second list shows how Satan has perverted the truth. Unfortunately, many Christians live in the second list.

GOD'S PERSPECTIVE OF THE TRUTH

1. God is sovereign (v5,9,11)
   I alone am God
   There is none beside me
   I have your best interest in mind

2. Election (v4)
   I love you
   I want you
   I choose you

3. Predestination (v5,11)
   I have preplanned your destiny

4. Adoption (v5)
   You have adult status in my family

5. Accepted in Christ (v6)
   You have been made acceptable
   You are highly favored

6. Redemption (v7)
   Christ paid the ransom for you

7. Forgiveness (v7)
   Christ paid your penalty
   You have been pardoned

8. Inheritance (v11)
   Christ is your inheritance

9. Saved (v13)
   You have an eternal salvation

10. Sealed (v13)
    The Holy Spirit is God's guarantee that what he has
    started, he will complete.

SATAN'S PERVERSION OF THE TRUTH

1. Concerning God's Sovereignty
   There are many gods
   You can be a god
   God is not concerned with you

2. Concerning Election
   You are unlovable
   You are unwanted
   You are left out

3. Concerning Predestination
   You have no future

4. Concerning Adoption
   You are an abandoned orphan

5. Concerning Acceptance
   You are unacceptable
   You are worthless

6. Concerning Redemption
   You have to earn your salvation
   You have to be good enough, and you can't be

7. Concerning Forgiveness
   You are under condemnation
   You still bear the guilt of your sins

8. Concerning Inheritance
   You are empty-handed
   You have nothing to look forward to
   You must focus on worldly things

9. Concerning Salvation
   You are lost

10. Concerning Sealing
    God will abandon you

How many times has the adversary used these perverted statements as weapons against you in the spiritual warfare? If we do not know the truth in these areas, we will fall for Satan's lie every time. The truth of the Word of God is for the benefit of the believer to be able to walk in faith and live a life that is pleasing to God. The 10 doctrines we have seen in this passage of

Scripture are solid spiritual rock that we can stand upon. They are the girdle of truth. Our adversary has no defense against these doctrines. He can only hope to deceive us concerning them. If he can win the battle of deceit, he needs no defense. He can win his battles on the ignorance of God's people. But as the Scripture says, when we know the truth, the truth will make us free.

The Bible is the truth, but simply picking up a Bible is not how the truth will make us free. We have to get into the Word. When we have gotten into the Word, we have to stay, or abide, in the Word. This is what it means to continue in the Word as Jesus said. We have to expose ourself to the truth by reading it. We have to read it so we can know it. Then we have to believe it. We have to come to some understanding of it so we can obey it. We have to guard the truth to keep the enemy from stealing it or diluting it. Finally, we have to give it away to others. Giving it away to others is the best way to keep it for ourselves.

We can be free of the devil's advantage over us when we know the truth, especially in the 10 areas we have mentioned. Knowing this truth takes away these particular weapons and methods of attack that the enemy uses against us. Did you get this? Knowing and standing on these truths will take away at least 10 weapons from the adversary's arsenal against us. And as we grow in Christ, this will encompass all of the truth of God's Word, not just these 10 doctrines. Therefore, study the truth. Come to grips with the truth. Embrace the truth. Stand on the truth. Wear the truth as the girdle and foundation of your spiritual strength, and you will see the enemy lose their advantage in your life. You will begin to win major battles against the enemy, clearing the way for you to walk a consistent life of faith unto the pleasing of God.

CHAPTER 3

THE BREASTPLATE OF RIGHTEOUSNESS

COMPREHENDING CORRECT DOCTRINE

and having on the breastplate of righteousness;
(Ephesians 6:14b)

The second half of Ephesians chapter one gives us our second piece of the whole armor of God, the breastplate of righteousness (1:15-23). We see it in verses 17 and 18 when Paul speaks of the spirit of wisdom and revelation in the knowledge of Christ and the eyes of our understanding being enlightened. Some versions of the Bible use the word heart for the word understanding, and the subject matter Paul talks about is clearly matters of the heart. And, which vital organ is protected by a breastplate? The heart, of course. Therefore, we conclude that we are in the realm of the breastplate of righteousness in this passage of Scripture.

This piece of the armor reveals two things. It shows us three things we need to know from God's perspective,

27

Allen L. Elder

and it shows us five weapons that our adversary uses against us when we do not know the truth and have not been made free by it.

In this portion of the text, there is one emphatic word, one word which stresses the critical issue at hand; the word enlightened. I call this the Christian's greatest need after salvation. My own paraphrase of the passage says, "I am asking the Spirit of God who lives in your spirit, to turn on the light in your heart that you might see three critical areas from God's point of view."

THREE THINGS TO SEE FROM GOD'S PERSPECTIVE

The three areas we need to see from God's point of view are these: the hope of his calling, the riches of the glory of his inheritance in the saints, and what is the exceeding greatness of his power to believers according to the working of his mighty power. These three areas really do get to the heart of the matter. We might be able to grasp them better by saying something like this, "God wants us to see from his point of view: His purpose for our life, how valuable we are to him, and how his power works in us and through us." Let's look a little closer.

When we speak of God's purpose for our life, we speak of it in two categories. First is God's general purpose for all of us. People often say, "I know I am here for a reason, I just don't know what it is." Well, the Bible tells us what this reason is. We do not have to wonder about it because the Bible is clear on this point. God's general purpose for every believer at this time in history is what we call the great commission. Most Christians think this phrase refers only to people who serve in Christian vocations such as pastors or missionaries. It has not dawned on so many Christians that this is God's general purpose for all of us. The great commission is God's command to make disciples of all

28

ethnic groups all over the world. This is the general purpose of God for all of us, not just pastors and missionaries. I always like to say that there are no exceptions, no exemptions, and no excuses for any believer to not be engaged in this purpose.

Next, we can talk about God's specific purpose for each one of us. This is the specific way each one of us will go about fulfilling God's general purpose to make disciples of the nations. God has specific work he wants us to do (Ephesians 2:10). He has placed a desire in our hearts (Ecclesiastes 3:11) that matches this work, and he has given us a spiritual gift (Romans 12:6-9) which equips us for the work. With a single idea, we can move out with this knowledge and begin our ministry which can make an impact on a global scale and accomplish the specific work God has in mind for us to do. This thing about purpose is the first thing we need to see from God's point of view.

The second thing we need to see from God's point of view is how valuable we are to God. Paul stated this as what the riches of the glory of his inheritance in the saints is all about. Usually when we hear the word inheritance, we immediately assume the Bible is speaking of the eternal inheritance we have awaiting us in heaven. We think of the glorious New Jerusalem with jasper walls, pearly gates, golden streets, and beautiful mansions. We think of crowns and rewards for our service on earth. We think of the fact that we will be there with Jesus for eternity with no possibility of things diminishing or ending. This is quite an inheritance to think about. It is real, it is ours, and it is on reserve for us in heaven. However, this is not the inheritance Paul is speaking of in Ephesians 1:18. He spoke of this inheritance in Ephesians 1:11. In Ephesians 1:18, Paul is not speaking of our inheritance in Christ, but of Christ's inheritance in us, his saints. These are two very different subjects. I love this verse in The Living

Bible which says, "I want you to realize that God has been made rich because we who are Christ's have been given to him!" This verse tells us that from God's point of view, we are very valuable to him. We are a treasure, and we are one of the reasons God is so rich. We are the inheritance of Christ. We are more valuable to him than we have ever begun to realize.

For the most part, most people believe that the real value of a thing can be seen in the price tag that is on the item. We go into a store and look at a jacket that we like and it either has a good price on it or it does not. If it is too high, we leave it there and go to another store, hoping to find a better price. On the other hand, if an item is scarce, and if we want it bad enough, we will pay a higher price than we might pay otherwise.

The principle is this: the true value of an item is not in the price tag that is on it, but is in what someone will actually pay for it. A five-cent baseball card may not be worth any more than that to us, but someone may pay $1,000.00 for it. The card is only as valuable as what someone actually pays for it.

Now ask yourself this question, "How valuable am I?" The answer to this question depends upon the person to whom the question is presented. If the question is presented to God, which is what Paul is trying to get us to do in this passage, the answer is incredible. What price did God pay for you? Jesus! This means that in the sight of God, each saint of God is very valuable, in fact, equal in value to Jesus because Jesus is the price that God paid for us. This is unbelievable to many of us. No wonder we need to see this truth from God's perspective.

Third, Paul said we need to see and know the power of God in us in which we can serve the Lord in our own specific way. In verse 19, Paul used four words for power. A fifth word is found in the great commission passage of Matthew 28:18-20. One word (exousia) means authority (Matthew 28:18); one word (ischys) is abiding power; one word (kratos) is applied power; one word (dunamis) is ability, and one word (energia) is action (Ephesians 1:19). When we put the words together, this is what we find. All authority (power) abides in me. When this power is applied to my situation, God gives me the ability to act. In other words, this is how God works through us as we yield ourselves to him. He does the work through us. And when we remove our hands from the work, the fingerprints of God are left behind upon it.

Notice the order of the three things we need to see from God's point of view: purpose, value, power. If we were writing Scripture apart from the inspiration of the Holy Spirit, we would probably place power at the front of the list. We want the power first. We do not want to have to do anything extra to get the power that we want. We want it for our use instantly in its full force and for whatever purpose for which we want to use it. This is exactly the reason that the power comes last. God is not going to manifest his power through us until we know the purpose for which it is to be used. Learn the purpose first and align with it. Live as a valued saint in the work of the Lord and you will find God's power at work through you in all that you do. This makes me want to see these things more and more from God's point of view.

FIVE WEAPONS

Not only do these three areas get to the heart of the matter, but they expose some of our adversary's gameplan against us. They uncover at least five weapons that the enemy uses against us, and in fact, uses very well. Let's name the five weapons: incognizance, insignificance, insecurity, insufficiency, and indifference. I guarantee you that at least one of these five weapons was and perhaps still is in the adversary's top weapons against you. I can say this because I have seen them used by the devil in the lives of believers for nearly 40 years of ministry. They are so effective because many believers do not even realize the weapons are being used on them.

Next, let's list the weapons and the effect they have in the life of the believer.

Incognizance results in a condition of (I don't know)
Insignificance results in a condition of (I cannot do anything)
Insecurity results in a condition of (I am nobody)
Insufficiency results in a condition of (I have nothing to use)
Indifference results in a condition of (I don't care)

Incognizance is another word for ignorance. Ignorance simply means that one does not know. This is why Jesus said we have to know the truth if we are to have any possibility of being made free by it. Perhaps the worst ignorance of all is to assume you know when you really do not know. True knowledge is rooted in truth. And knowing the truth is the first step toward freedom. This would have to mean that the purposeful use of nontruth would have to be bondage of some kind or the other.

Notice this key aspect of truth. Before truth is a creed or a grouping of words and statements of any kind, it is a person. Jesus said, "I am the truth" (John 14:6). Truth finds it substance in the person of Jesus Christ. The closer we get to Jesus, the closer we get to truth. The farther from Jesus we move, the farther from truth we will find ourselves. Therefore, truth can be found in Jesus Christ and in the Word of God that God has given us. This makes the Bible the rule and guide for our life. The Word of God is the revealer of that which is true and that which is false. If you want to know the truth and be made free by it, get to know Jesus through the Word of God and in your relationship with him. This knowing Jesus and the truth in relation to him is the reason Paul said we need the Holy Spirit to turn the light on in our heart that we might see from God's perspective, indeed, that we might know the truth in some key areas of life.

The adversary uses very effectively in the life of many believers the weapon of insignificance. We look at what seems to be a world gone completely insane and we hear the enemy say, "There is nothing you can do. You are only one person in a sea of billions of people. You are so far removed from the epicenter of world conditions and events. You and the little you might do are so insignificant. You could never make any real difference in a situation so far out of reach as the world's situation is today. So why bother?"

The condition of insignificance brings us to the place that we ignore the conditions in the world around us and just seek the best life we can find in the world as far away from these conditions as possible. We are not as crazy, perhaps, as the people and world around us, so if we will just ignore it, we can live a pretty comfortable and happy life on our own terms. Instead of doing the little we can do to make some difference, we do nothing except live a good life apart from the chaos in the world.

The problem with living this way is that the little we can do never gets done. The little we can do, when it is touched and blessed by the power of the Holy Spirit, can become exceeding abundantly above all we can ask or think. The presence of the Holy Spirit negates insignificance. As the old song used to say, "Little is much when God is in it." Jesus said that even a cup of water in his name would bring reward which is the result of making a significant impact. If the adversary

33

can get you to believe there is nothing you can do in the world to make a difference, you will do nothing in the world to make a difference. Insignificance is found in the devil's camp, not in God's camp. The little boy with a sack lunch near the Sea of Galilee found this to be true (John 6:9), and so did the thousands of people who ate from his lunch that day.

Insecurity is the next weapon in the devil's arsenal. He wants us to believe that we are of no value to anyone, worthless and useless. Usually to get us to buy into this lie, the enemy will see to it that some person in our life, someone who should be very close to us otherwise, will do something to make us feel useless. And they will keep reminding us that, according to them, we are worthless. Surely if certain people tell us we are worthless, why would we ever think that God would have any other opinion of us either? So, we live our life, feeling worthless to everyone, even to God.

When we are insecure, we will go about trying to do things we would not generally do, or to be someone we are not, all in an effort to try to make ourself valuable in some way to someone who considers us to be useless. More often than not, our efforts will not achieve for us that which we want, and we end up disappointed all over again, and the insecurity continues and grows.

Real security is found in only one place: in God. No wonder Paul exhorts us that we see ourselves in this area from God's point of view. Just what is God's point of view in this area, you may ask. His point of view, as we have already stated, is that to him, we are worth Jesus. This one fact should clear up any issue that any believer has regarding his worth. In this world, we may not be worth much to certain people, but to the One that really matters, to God, we are worth everything. If we will embrace our value in this one place and person, it does not matter who else may think we are worthless, the problem of insecurity is solved, and the weapon of insecurity used by the devil against us is silenced.

Yet another weapon in the devil's schemes against us is that of insufficiency. The problems in the world are too big and the resources I have to help are too small. I have insufficient funds to take on the world's needs, and to solve the world's problems, so here again, I will do nothing. There are two things the devil does not want us to know. He does not want us to know that God has all the resources we will ever need to do the work he has given us to do. And, he does not want us to know that God has these resources ready to meet our needs as we encounter them in our ministries. There are two keys to getting these resources. We must align ourselves with the person, purpose, and plan of God in the world, or as Jesus said, to seek first the kingdom of heaven. And, we must keep ourselves humble before the Lord, seeing to it that pride is never allowed to stand in our way, because God resists the proud but gives grace to the humble. The all-sufficiency of Christ must replace our insufficiency.

In the fifth place, there is the weapon of indifference. To be indifferent is to simply not care. This is the compound result of having been victimized by the other four weapons along the way. When we have tried and failed time after time, we get to the place where we just don't care about the issues at hand or about how we can make any impact in any of these areas. Indifference is the condition of many believers in the church today; they just don't care.

The remedy for indifference is to get a fresh look and understanding of what it is that God wants his followers to do in the world. In Ephesians 4:1, Paul tells us to walk worthy of the vocation into which we have been called. If you want or need something to care about, care about the work God has in mind for you to do in this world. You are the only one who can do the works

God wants you to do. How much time have you wasted to this point? There is no way to know how much time you have left to work. The night is coming when no one can work. Get involved and do what you can do for the rest of your life from this point in time. Redeem the time. Number your days and apply your heart to wisdom. Do what you can with whatever time you have left.

The serpent was more subtle than any beast of the field. He is cunning and crafty. His wiles are effective. He is a master at laying and setting a trap. The five weapons we have just mentioned are five of his most effective ones. You can neutralize them, and all of his weaponry for that matter, simply by knowing the truth, understanding it, and being obedient to it, and staying with it. All of these target areas are matters of the heart. "Guard your heart", Solomon wrote, "for out of it are the issues of life" (Proverbs 4:23). Wearing the breastplate of righteousness is the way to guard your heart in this whole armor of God lifestyle.

CHAPTER 4

THE SHOES OF THE PREPARATION OF THE GOSPEL OF PEACE

WALKING IN CORRECT DOCTRINE

And your feet shod with the preparation of the gospel of peace;
(Ephesians 6:15)

The whole armor of God is a lifestyle, a way of life. It requires all seven pieces of the armor to live this lifestyle. The first three pieces show us how to begin to walk by faith. We start with knowing the truth, understanding the truth we know, and then putting shoes on our faith by walking out the truth in our daily life. We have to obey, or live up to the truth, if it is going to do for us what the truth can do.

Chapters two and three of Ephesians make up the third piece of the whole armor of God; the shoes of the preparation of the gospel of peace. Again, the word preparation indicates that we are still in the beginning phases of something, in this case, learning to walk consistently by faith. This part of the whole armor of God lifestyle is where we apply the truth to our life. We do not simply talk about the truth, we live by it. We order our life by it. We live by the gospel that we profess to believe. Through this part of the process, we are walking in and walking out the gospel. This piece of the armor gives us a panoramic view of our life, from the peril of being lost to the potential and possibility of making an impact in the world for Christ in an everlasting way. There are four frames which make up this panoramic view. Take a careful look at each frame.

WHAT IT IS TO BE LOST

When we break down the world's population into its most basic parts, we find that there are really only two kinds of people in the world, those who are lost and those who are saved. The terms saved and lost may be new terms to some readers so let's define them. To be saved is to have believed on the Lord Jesus Christ in the heart and to have said to God that you believe on Jesus. The person in whom God has done this work of grace is a new creature in Christ. He has been released from God's condemnation, from the penalty of sin, and has been declared righteous in the sight of God through the finished work of Jesus Christ at the cross when he shed his blood and died to redeem his people from their sin. To be lost is to still be in a state of spiritual death, separation from God, under God's condemnation, and unable to save oneself. This is the condition into which everyone was put when man fell into sin in Genesis chapter three. We all come into the world in the lost condition. These are the only two spiritual categories in God's sight in which a person may be found.

A difference-maker in the life of one who is saved is the truth about his new standing before God. The Bible makes plain what this difference is. Our definitions in the preceding paragraph show some of these differences. Other details of the difference can be found throughout the Bible. The problem in the lives of many

Christians is that they do not know what the Bible says about these two spiritual conditions, saved and lost. One reason some Christians have such a problem with what the Bible says about salvation is that they do not know and realize what a desperate condition it is to be lost. Paul presents some of the details of the lost condition in Ephesians chapter two. It will do us good to look at this condition, making us thankful that God has delivered us from it, and motivating us to be more intentional about sharing the gospel with those around us who are still lost.

Paul mentions eight facets to the lost condition in Ephesians 2:1-3. Any one of them is a terrible condition in and of itself. Compounded, they make up the hopeless condition of being lost and show the reason that the grace of God is our only hope of salvation. Outside of Christ we were:

1 – DEAD
(v1) And you hath he quickened, who were dead in trespasses and sins;

If we did not have the other seven facets of the lost condition, this one would spell our situation completely by itself. What can anything or anyone do that is dead? This death is a spiritual one. This is the one God primarily had in mind when he said to Adam regarding the tree of the knowledge of good and evil, "The day you eat of the fruit of this tree, you will die" (Genesis 2:7). The death was first and foremost a spiritual death. God left the spirit of man and man died in the spirit. Because of this death, the man is separated from God, under God's condemnation, and is unable to save himself or to even contribute to his salvation. This is man's condition as God sees it. Of course, because man can still breath, walk, think, and do things he wants to do in this life, man does not consider his spiritual condition until and unless he hears the gospel of Jesus Christ. Then, he only considers it as God is at work in his heart. Otherwise, he is stone cold dead as far as Almighty God is concerned.

2 – DEPRAVED
(2a) Wherein in time past ye walked

This part of the passage tells us that we walked, or lived, in this condition of spiritual death. Everything a person does while he is in the lost condition is in the realm of spiritual death as God sees it. Even the good things he does in the eyes of men account for nothing before God. It is all sin and in the condition of spiritual death. This is the condition the old theologians referred to as total depravity. Our total being was affected by the fall into sin. In this condition, apart from the restraint of the Holy Spirit, there is no limit to the depths of depravity that people can stoop. This does not mean they will stoop to the lowest sins, but that they are capable of doing so, and they would do so were it not for the restraint of the Holy Spirit. Apart from the saving grace of God, there is no escape from this awful depravity.

3 – DISTRESSED
(2b) according to the course of this world,

People often say, "This is the twenty-first century. Things are different now. Man has gotten so much better and these things do not apply to man in our day and time." Unfortunately, this is not true. For the lost to walk or live in depravity is just how it is. This is the course of this world now that it is in a fallen condition. It makes no difference what century a person may be born; these are the realities of the fallen world. These things are still just as true today as they were when

Adam first sinned. These conditions will remain until God creates the new heaven and the new earth where righteousness will prevail. Until then, these distressed conditions will remain.

4 – DEMON ENERGIZED
(2c) according to the prince of the power of the air, the spirit that now worketh

When we were lost, a spirit of antichrist operated in all of is. Thank God, this evil spirit was not allowed a free reign in our life. If it had been, we would have done a lot worse things than we did as lost people. Thankfully, God did restrain it. Demon-energized people are not all maniacal. They do not all kill people and tear buildings apart from one end to the other. In the least, they are simply anti-Christ. They refuse to follow Christ on their own and seek to live their life in their own way.

5 – DISOBEDIENT
(2d) in the children of disobedience:

In the lost condition, as God sees it, all of life is disobedience. There may be the sweetest person you have ever known who feeds the hungry and helps the homeless, but if this person has never been born again, they are living a life of disobedience toward God. To be disobedient is to be unbelieving and uncompliant. This is another reason we need the grace of God to act upon our life. The lost spirit does not believe in God and cannot do the things God wants it to do of its own accord. We need God to rescue and release us from this bondage.

6 – DOMINATED BY THE TOTALLY DEPRAVED NATURE
(3a) Among whom also we all had our conversation in times past in the lusts of our flesh,

The flesh, the totally depraved nature, was the realm in which we lived as a lost person. This nature, apart from several restraints that God put into our life, would have its own way which is contrary to the ways of God. We all lived in this way. No one has been immune to it. We pursued the desires of our flesh. This was our way of life without God living in our spirit.

7 – DIRECTED BY OUR EMOTIONS
(3b) fulfilling the desires of the flesh and of the mind;

In the lost condition, living in the flesh is the way of life. When we were lost, we were controlled and instigated by our thoughts and by the desires of the flesh. We responded and reacted to things from our feelings rather than from faith and from a spiritual perspective. Thoughts and feelings can be cruel partners in life if they are unbridled. In the flesh, they are of course, unbridled, and this is what makes them so dangerous. In the fleshly realm, thoughts get us into certain situations and feelings can keep us there. Hence, they are chief contributors to the inescapable life of the flesh and of sin. As Paul queried, "Who shall deliver me from the body of this death?" And the only answer is Jesus Christ.

8 – DEFENSELESS
(3c) and were by nature the children of wrath, even as others.

The lost are already under the wrath and condemnation of God. They are the enemies of God.

God has set himself against them. A condition of enmity exists between them and God. Unless God changes the situation, more wrath from God is in store for them both in this life an in eternity to come. There is no defense from the wrath of God. If the lost condition continues, those who are lost will bear the full brunt of the wrath of God.

What a terrible thing to be lost. As if verses 1-3 are not bad enough, add to them the facts given in verses 11-12. We were Gentiles in the flesh, the Uncircumcision, we were without Christ, aliens from the commonwealth of Israel, strangers from the covenants and promises, having no hope, and without God in the world. It just cannot get any worse than this. This is the lost condition that many Christians do not understand to be as hopeless as it really is. The only remedy for the lost condition is the work Jesus did to redeem and rescue his people from their sin. So, in the second frame of our panoramic view, let's consider what it is to be saved.

WHAT IT IS TO BE SAVED

After this dark and gloomy condition of being lost come some of the most brilliant and glorious words in all of Scripture; "but God who is rich in mercy." Speaking for believers in Jesus Christ, God has saved our lost souls. Notice the three things he did in this salvation. First, he raised us up, he resurrected us from spiritual death. The same miracle of resurrection that occurred three days after Christ's crucifixion has occurred in us. Salvation, the new birth, being saved, is nothing short of resurrection from the dead. Second, he quickened us, he reanimated us with Christ. Christ now lives his life in us. We are dead and our life is hidden with Christ in God. This is Paul's mystery within a mystery of Colossians 1, Christ in you, the hope of glory.   Third, we are seated with Christ, spiritually speaking, in heaven. This means nothing can change this condition into which we have been born again. This passage, like many others, confirms the eternal security of our salvation in Christ Jesus.

The way God has done this is by grace and through faith. Some people may say that the grace is God's part of salvation, and the faith is our part of salvation, but this is not true. This passage tells us that both the grace and the faith are gifts from God to us. The truth is that God graciously grants us the faith to believe in him. If he did not do this, we have already established from verses 1-3 that we could not do it ourselves. If we could do it ourselves, it would be works and not grace. Paul said plainly, it, salvation, is not of works but by grace through faith which both come from God. God also did this that he might show through us and through the eternal ages his rich grace and kindness toward us.

Next we see that God has a purpose for our life on earth. He has had this purpose in his mind concerning us from before he made the world. He has work for us to do. He is presently in the process of conforming us to the image of Christ so that we might do the work he has planned for us to do. He is making a masterpiece out of our life in the way we reflect Christ and serve him according to his good pleasure and by his design.

What a contrast between the lost condition and the saved condition. God has taken us from a hopeless condition apart from him to a condition of present usefulness and of eternal glory. Let's look at the next two frames in this panoramic view in Scripture to see more about the preparation we need in order to walk a consistent life of faith.

THE CHURCH

The church is Christ's body, building, and bride in the world today. He made it out of two kinds of people; believing Jews and believing Gentiles, all the seed of Abraham. He equipped the church and gave it a job to do when he ascended back to heaven. He commissioned every believer in the church to engage in the making of disciples in all nations until he returns for us all. This one task encompasses everything we do in the church. And the ministries we do in the world are part of the work and ministry of the church. The church is built upon Christ himself and nothing will prevail against it. The church, the Word of God, and the true disciples of Christ are the only things that will remain when the earth itself has passed away.

OUR POTENTIAL IMPACT

In the final frame of the panoramic view given by Paul, we see that when we put on the shoes of the preparation of the gospel of peace, we are aligning ourself for the impact that can come from our life if we will do the work God has given us to do. Just because we have been saved, brought out of darkness into the marvelous light of God, does not mean that we will automatically realize our impact in the world. It will not happen on its own. We have to prepare for the impact by putting on the shoes of the gospel of peace and we have to walk out our faith in front of the people with whom we come into contact in the world in our daily experience of life. It is in the context of the church that the individuals whom God has saved out of the lost condition fulfill the purpose that God has for their life. All the dimensions of the faith and of the church, the width, length, height, and depth, can be explored and extended on the condition that we find, follow, and fulfill the purpose of God for our life in and through his church.

It is in our connection to the church that the potential of the impact of our life can be realized in the world in which we live. Paul said our life can have an impact in the world through the church for the glory of God all the way until the end of time if we walk out our faith according to the Word of God. This is the end result of the whole armor of God lifestyle. The ultimate reason to be protected by the armor is so that we can reach our potential, making our personal impact in the world, and accomplishing the mission the Lord has given us in the world.

As we prepare to walk by faith and fulfill the purpose of God for our life, let us get this four-frame panoramic view fixed in our mind. We were lost, we have been saved, we are now a part of the church, the body of Christ, and we have the potential to make a real spiritual impact in the world for Christ to the last person on earth until the end of time if we will walk consistently by faith which is what it means to wear the whole armor of God.

It is a long way from having the possibilities of world impact laid before us and to reaching them. To reach them, we have to put on the shoes of the gospel of peace and begin to walk. Our impact may not look like much when we begin. We may wobble on the axles from this side of the road to that side. We may fall down and get back up time and time again. We may even start and stop a few times. But if we will stick with it and keep on walking, we will finally see the travail of our souls at some point down the road. The enemy will give us every reason to quit. We may even want to quit from time to time. But we have to remember Paul's word of encouragement, in due season we will reap the harvest if we do not grow tired and quit (Galatians 6:9). Let us get our shoes on and start walking by faith.

CHAPTER 5

THE SHIELD OF FAITH

LIVING A CONSISTANT LIFE OF FAITH

*Above all, taking the shield of faith, wherewith ye shall
be able to quench all the fiery darts of the wicked
(Ephesians 6:16)*

The fourth piece of the whole armor of God, and the
balance point in life, is the shield of faith. The portion
of Paul's letter to the Ephesians dealing with the shield
of faith is found from chapter 4:1 to chapter 5:2. Now
that we have our shoes on our feet, we can walk worthy
of the vocation wherewith we are called. The walk can
be consistent, and the walk is by and in faith.

The righteousness of God is revealed from faith to
faith, and the just shall live by faith (Rom 1:17). We
walk by faith and not by sight (2 Corinthians 5:7).
Without faith, it is impossible to please God (Hebrews,
11:6). And by taking up the shield of faith as a way of
life, we will be able to quench, or extinguish, or put out,
ALL of the fiery darts of the wicked one (Ephesians
6:16).

ALL of the fiery darts of the wicked one. ALL means
every last one of them. ALL means there is not one fiery
dart or flaming missile of the adversary that can get

47

through to me unless I am not walking consistently by and in faith. If a fiery dart has gotten through, struck my life and done its damage, this is evidence that I was not properly wearing the whole armor of God. It is not evidence that the whole armor of God could not do its duty against a certain weapon of the enemy but rather that I was walking in the flesh instead of walking by faith. Even as I write these words, I am encouraged that the possibility exists that the shield of faith that comes by living consistently a life of faith will stop every weapon the devil can launch against me even before it can begin to do its damage.

ENVIRONMENT

This consistent walk of faith is done in a certain environment, and the environment is that of oneness or unity. Keeping the unity of the Spirit in the bond of peace is the environment we are to walk in and the goal toward which we are to strive as a member of the church of Jesus Christ. There is one body, one Spirit, one hope, one Lord, one faith, one baptism, one God, and one Father. This oneness, this unity, is the environment in which we are to live out our life of walking consistently by faith.

This unity is priceless. The Psalmist spoke of how good and how pleasant it is for brothers to dwell together in unity (Psalm 133:1). This unity is also a target of the adversary and is constantly under attack. The enemy knows how good and how pleasant the environment of unity is for the people of God. When Christian brothers and sisters live and work together as one unit, as one body, they are an unstoppable force; there is nothing out of their reach when they walk together with God in this way. This kind of church is an indestructible enemy of the adversary. The enemy must target and attack unity because division weakens the body of Christ. Therefore, we must endeavor to keep the unity, the oneness.

EQUIPPING

God has provided two indispensable things for us which contribute to, or which produce unity. They are doctrine and purpose. God has also provided teaching pastors for the church to use each of these tools to produce unity which in turn, helps maintain the unity and oneness of the body of Christ.

Doctrine is that body of truth which lays out the standards of God to and for his people. The doctrine is that which brings us into the unity of the faith and builds us up to reach the stature of Christ, keeping us from being tossed about by false teachings which undermine the unity of the body.

We have seen those believers upon whom this doctrinal attack has had its effect. They walk, or live, in the vanity of their mind. Their understanding is darkened. They are alienated from the life of God through ignorance. They are past feeling. They are given over to filthy ways of living and to greed. In short, they live as if they have never been saved at all. Instead of being a global witness for Christ in the world, they become a poster child for everything a believer in Christ ought not to be.

Purpose of heart is also a producer of and preserver of the unity of the church. Teaching pastors equip us for the daily work of the ministry, or the individual, specific purposes to which we have been called. The fulfillment of these purposes is that which builds up the body of Christ. When we are all in our specific place within the body and fulfilling our specific role in the body, the body is healthy, growing, and effective. Again, there is no Satanic force greater than the unified body of Christ.

49

EXERCISE

To maintain the unity of the faith means that every believer has an exercise to perform. The exercise is simple; put off the old man and put on the new man. This simple exercise is easier said than done. It is completely impossible in the strength of the flesh. The more we do it with the help of the Holy Spirit, the easier it becomes because it is becoming a part of our way of life. And it is the only thing that will produce that which we need in this context.

Putting off the old man is simply eliminating everything from our life that has to do with the lost condition outside of Jesus Christ. Put away lying. Stop sinning in anger. Stop letting the day end and entering into other days by being angry with others and within yourself. Stop allowing the devil to have his way in your life. Stop stealing. Stop being stingy. Stop being non-productive. Stop talking foolishly. Stop tearing others down with hurtful words. Stop grieving the Holy Spirit of God who lives within you. Do away with bitterness. Stop trying to get back at others, giving them what you think they deserve. Stop being malicious, heard-hearted, hateful, and unforgiving. Stop allowing the works and ways of the devil to be manifest in your life. This is putting off the old man and it is an exercise we must do daily.

Putting off the old man without putting on the new man is fruitless. We do not overcome sin simply by battling it, but by replacing it. And, we replace it with the new man in Christ. Put on the new man is the other half of this important daily exercise. To put on the new man is to be renewed in the spirit of the mind. This renewed mind allows us to live and walk in righteousness and true holiness. Put on the new man by speaking the truth, being honest, working as God has given you the ability, using words that build up people, pleasing God in any way you possibly can. The contrast between the old man and the new man is obvious. It is not hard to tell the difference.

EVIDENCE

And the difference will be evident to all who observe your way of life. Putting on the new man, walking in the Spirit, living a consistent life of faith shows people that you are a follower of Christ not only in word, but also in deed. The result of this way of life is that the love of God will be observed, felt, and experienced in and through your life. The love of God will not be something we have to consciously try to manufacture. It will flow from us naturally, rather supernaturally. This is that which makes and means that it is real, giving it the effect God intends his love through us to have on others. They will recognize the realness of it, and some will be drawn to it. People will see the difference Christ has made in your life and cause some of them to want as much in their own life. This is the kind of life that witnesses of the life-changing power of God. It is more evidence of the truth of the Bible and of the difference Christ makes in our lives.

It is when we sporadically live this way, or when we do not live this way at all that the fiery darts of the enemy light up or lives. Doing what it takes to put off the old man and to put on the new man again reduces the arsenal of the enemy against our life. Those who walk consistently by faith enjoy the protection of the whole armor of God and have less problem with the adversary and less destruction in their life caused by them. This way of life is pleasing to God because we are living in the way made possible by the sacrifice of Christ on the cross, and this is a sweet-smelling savor unto God.

Allen L. Elder

CHAPTER 6

THE HELMET OF SALVATION

KEEPING YOUR MIND CLEAN

And take the helmet of salvation
(Ephesians 6:17a)

The next piece of the whole armor of God is the helmet of salvation. The helmet is protection for the vital organ we call the brain. People generally associate the mind with the brain however they are two different things. They work together but are different entities. Paul speaks of the mind, or heart, from chapter 5:3 to chapter 6:9. In these verses, we are clearly dealing with matters of the heart, or mind, and thoughts. Thus, we have the need for protection for our minds and this protection is provided through the helmet of salvation. Our new birth has made it possible for us to be relieved from the fleshly mind by being given a new mind, the mind of Christ. Here again, Paul is using the example of a soldier's armor, the helmet in this case, to explain what it is to continue to walk in the Spirit, or to walk by faith.

Allen L. Elder

TWO MINDS

The believer has two minds, the mind of the flesh, and the mind of Christ. With either mind, we think, feel, and choose to do the things we do. In this way, the mind and the brain work together to move the body to action. When we think with the carnal mind, the brain moves the body to produce carnal actions. When we think with the new mind, the Spirit stimulates the brain to move the body to do the things which are pleasing to God.

The flesh was killed at Calvary but it can still animate our body if we choose to think with it. The daily struggle for the believer is deciding which mind with which he is going to think. The carnal mind is at war with God. To think out of it brings results which are against God. Carnal thinking results in fleshy living and it is impossible to please God in the flesh. Therefore, we must put to death the carnal deeds of the body and we do this by choosing not to think with the carnal mind and to think with the mind of Christ.

Jeremiah 17:9 says the heart, that is the carnal mind, is deceitful above all things and desperately wicked. Jesus said that out of the carnal mind come evil thoughts and sinful actions (Matthew 15:19). It is this carnal mind and its thinking which must be brought into the captivity of Jesus Christ (2 Corinthians 10:3-5). It would be impossible to bring every individual thought of the carnal mind, one at a time, under the captivity of Christ every single day and still be able to function in life. The thing to do is to submit the total carnal mind to Christ as a whole and think with the new mind. Individual carnal thoughts can be arrested as necessary as they arise throughout each day in their attempt to keep us from thinking with the mind of Christ.

As a result of salvation in Jesus, the believer has a new mind, the mind of Christ (1 Corinthians 2:16). It is this new mind energized by the indwelling Spirit of God that quickens our mortal bodies to do the things God wants us to do (Romans 8:11). Choosing to think with the mind of Christ is wearing the helmet of salvation, keeping the mind clean of impure thoughts, and thinking on whatsoever things are true, honest, just, pure, lovely, of good report, virtuous, and praiseworthy (Philippians 4:8). These are the things upon which we need to think.

OUR THINKING AND OUR RELATIONSHIPS

It is amazing to see from this passage of Scripture that our relationships with the people in our lives are directly connected to our thinking. First, we are given six practices that will stop in our life when we get our thinking in order by wearing the helmet of salvation. The helmet of salvation will keep our mind clean by stopping our thoughts on the sins which rise out of the carnal mind (5:3-5). We will stop being deceived by vain, or empty words (5:6). We will stop joining with others in their sinful actions (5:7). We will stop fellowshipping in darkness (5:11). We will stop misunderstanding the will of God (5:17). And we will stop being controlled by anything other than the Holy Spirit (5:18). What a powerful and effective tool this helmet of salvation is to the child of God. Thinking out of the mind of Christ will break these afore mentioned barriers to good relationships.

When we get and keep our mind clean with the helmet of salvation, the relationships which matter most can become all they were meant to be in our experience. First, we can have a right relationship with our self (5:6-21). A clean mind will allow us to enjoy the good things God has prepared for those who are in

Christ Jesus. We will think like the saints of God are supposed to think, free of depraved, sinful thoughts. We will live and walk as children of light, doing the things which are pleasing to God. We will make the most of the time which God gives us. We will encourage ourselves with spiritual songs and we will be submissive one to another. The carnal mind can never produce these things.

The clean mind by way of the helmet of salvation also contributes to a right relationship between husband and wife (5:21-33). When we simply wear the helmet of salvation, our marriage relationships can develop supernaturally. We will find ourselves doing the things we need to do for our mate, without having to make ourselves do them. This relieves us from the struggle and from the effort which is not always out of the right motivation. In this way, we can experience marriage on the highest level.

The clean mind also effects the relationships between parents and children (6:1-4). Parents can be all they were meant to be for their children. And children can be all they were meant to be for their parents. There does not have to be the wars in the home, pitting one parent against another, one parent siding with the children against the other parent, or wars between siblings. Home truly can be sweet when our relationships are submitted to and governed by the word of God.

The helmet of salvation, a clean mind and right thinking, also has an effect on our relationships at work, the other place where we spend most of our time during the week (6:5-9). Employees can be what they need to be toward their employers and employers can be what they should be to their employees.

What a great thing it would be to have all of, or many of, our relationships to be the best they could be. This is possible through wearing the helmet of salvation and keeping our mind clean. There is a direct connection from the thoughts of our mind to our relationships with other people. Some of the problems in our relationships are caused by uncontrolled, unrighteous thoughts. Keeping our mind clean and controlling our thoughts contributes greatly to the health of these relationships. What a simple fix this is for those Christians who struggle with relationship problems day after day.

Allen L. Elder

CHAPTER 7

THE SWORD OF THE SPIRIT

COMBATTING THE ENEMY

and the sword of the Spirit, which is the word of God
(Ephesians 6:17b)

The sword of the spirit is the piece of the whole armor of God where we do something akin to hand-to-hand combat with the enemy. These are those times after the enemy has been frustrated by the impenetrable armor of God that they launch an all-out assault or a desperate attempt to try to destroy the child of God who is walking consistently by faith. These are those times when we have to withstand and do all to stand toe to toe with the adversary in the evil day (6:13). The attack of the enemy may be confined to one of the seven areas of the whole armor of God lifestyle, or it may be some combination of the seven areas, or it may be a conglomeration of all seven areas at once. Whatever the attack may be, we have the sword of the spirit with which to respond.

Allen L. Elder

REMEMBER THE APPROACH

The first thing to do as we respond to the enemy in spiritual warfare is to remember the approach Scripture tells us to take in this critical area of the Christian life. We spoke of this approach in chapter one, and (6:10-12) gives us the approach. First, we approach the enemy in the strength and power of the Lord. It is in the Lord and in his power that we find the strength we need for our spiritual battles. Next, we approach the enemy clothed in the whole armor of God. Again, the whole armor of God is a way of life. It is not magic words which give us instant protection when we encounter the adversary. When it is a way of life, we find ourselves having the protection we need from the enemy at all times. Finally, we approach our spiritual battles fully knowing who our enemy actually is. The enemy is the demons who sided with Satan in his revolt against God in heaven. This three-fold approach is the way to victory over our spiritual enemy.

THE SWORD OF THE SPIRIT IS THE WORD OF GOD

The sword of the spirit is the rhema of God. Rhema is the word of God for a specific situation. Going through this life, God will speak to us and we have to listen for and to the voice of God. He speaks to us as we go about daily life by the rhema word. We may not always have an open Bible before us as we go about the business of daily living. The God who indwells us will speak to us, directing us into the world about us. When God speaks a rhema word to us, he will always speak in alignment with the written Word of God, the logos. We can know that we have heard from God by submitting the rhema word to the logos Word. If the word we have heard does not align with the Word that is written, we

60

can be sure the God did not give us that word. It had to come from the adversary.

The Word of God, the Bible, is the only tangible thing we have on earth which connects us to our Father in heaven. Over the years, I have found that the one thing which makes the most difference in the life of those I have tried to disciple is to get them into the Bible. Getting people into the Bible for themselves changes their total perspective and thus, their life.

Let me suggest six responsibilities we have in relation to the Word of God. First, we simply need to read it. It is amazing the number of Christians I have encountered who seem to think they can get through life, live the Christian life, and do the things that God requires and that please him without having a regular connection with the Bible. It is the Bible which verifies everything else in life for us. We have to read it so that we can know what God has said, and what God requires of us as his followers. There is no short cut or substitute for it at all. One thing we have done to get people into the Bible is to start a Bible reading group. We started at Genesis 1 and are reading through the Bible, one chapter per day. Once per month, we meet as a group and discuss what we have read and what we are learning. This has proven to be a great experience for everyone in the group.

Next, we need to study the Word of God. We can all collectively study the Word of God for our entire lives and never even scratch the surface of the depth of the riches within the Word. The study of the Word shows us everything we need to know about life and godliness so we can live a life well pleasing to the Lord. The object in being a student of the Word is not just to collect knowledge, although we will do this, but it is to know the God who gave us the Bible in a personal and intimate way. In knowing him, we also get to know our self and can surrender all that we know about us to all that we know about him so that we can decrease, and he can increase in and through our life in the same way that he did in the life of John the Baptist in the Bible.

When we study the Word of God, we find those words, phrases, verses, or passages which speak to our heart and demand a closer look. To take the closer look, we meditate on those pieces of interest that we have found. We think over them and we think through them to extract as much nectar from them as we possibly can for the feeding of our soul.

As we meditate on the Word of God, going over and over it in our heart, we find ourselves becoming familiar with the Word and even memorizing it. Memorizing the Word can keep us from sin, can allow us to meditate more on portions of the Bible, and gives the Holy Spirit Scripture that he can bring to our memory as we need it in the everyday occurrences of life.

When we have obtained a good base of the Word in our life, we find it easier and easier to rely upon the Word, making us confident in its truth. We base our life upon it. We stand on it in times of trouble. It helps us to voice our praise to God in our worship. It teaches us what to do and how to do it in our service for God. Relying upon the Word helps to remove any reliance upon anything other than the Word in our life.

Finally, having the Word in our heart means we can wield it against our adversary when we are under spiritual attack. When Jesus was proven to be the sinless Son of God in the wilderness, when he was attacked by the devil, his answer was always, "It is written," and he quoted an appropriate Scripture for the area of attack in which he was under. The enemy knows the Word and uses it against the believer. As believers, we should know the Word and use it against the enemy. It is one of the things for which they have no defense.

When we live the consistent life of faith, we eliminate many of the enemy's weapons they can use against us. This can at times bring guerrilla attacks into our life from the enemy. They hit us fast and hard out of nowhere, ambushes, blindside attacks, sabotage, raids, and the like. This kind of warfare demands that we stand our ground against the enemy, wielding the sword of the spirit which is the word of God. The old soldiers of World War II have said to a man that the worst kind of fighting was the hand-to-hand combat in which at times they had to engage. Thankfully, our warfare is not on this level every day, but it is comforting to know that when we have to engage the enemy at close quarters, we have a superior weapon that can get the job done. We have the Word of God, and our enemy is powerless against it.

Allen L. Elder

CHAPTER 8

PRAYER

COMMUNING WITH GOD

*Praying always with all prayer and supplication in the
Spirit, and watching thereunto with all perseverance
and supplication for all saints
(Ephesians 6:18)*

The last piece of the whole armor of God, prayer, is the
piece that is often not thought of as a piece of armor,
consequently it gets left out of the list. Every piece of
the armor is important, but this is the one that speaks
of our communion with God. This is the place in the
protection cycle where we use our privilege of direct
access to our heavenly Father, settling into our personal
relationship with God in prayer. I like to think of this
piece of the armor, and of my experience of it, as the
green pastures, the still waters, the soul restoration, the
paths of righteousness for his name's sake, the
prepared banquet table, the anointing oil, and the
overflow of the goodness and mercy of God of which
David spoke in the twenty-third Psalm. This is the place
where we find the comfort we need, especially after an
intense, toe to toe battle with the enemy. The prayer
piece of the armor is spoken of from 6:18 to 6:24.

WARFARE PRAYING

In these verses, Paul identifies four facets of warfare prayer. First, prayer is an act of worship. When we face off with the enemy, sometimes worship is the farthest thing from our mind. However, it ought to be the closest thing to our mind. There is no greater need and no greater time to worship the one and only true and living God than when the enemy is trying to close in upon us. Worshipping God is one thing the adversary cannot do any more. God inhabits the praise of his people and when God comes on the scene, the enemy has to leave. Worship is not only an action that we do in adoration to and toward God, but it clears the atmosphere in which we are in of the presence of evil spirits. Prayer is the vehicle through which we gain these spiritual benefits and blessings.

Second, warfare praying is the business of supplication, or bringing our requests to God. There may never be a time when our prayers are more raw or more real and to the point than during a time of warfare. At these times, we do not have time for selfish requests. We do not have time to waste in asking amiss for something to consume upon our own carnal desires. We are in need of God to do exactly what is needed at the moment, therefore we are focused upon the need of the moment, whether that need is for ourselves or for someone else.

Third, we may even get to the place where we do not know anymore what to ask for or how to pray in the situation. This is where the Holy Spirit helps us by praying exactly for what we need. He knows more than we know what to ask for on our behalf. What a comfort it is to know that when I have reached the end of my praying, the Holy Spirit picks it up from there and prays with complete understanding, translating my wordlessness, deep desires, and inner groanings into eloquent prayers before the Father. This is indeed prayer that gets the job done.

Finally, warfare praying is watching and being vigilant in our praying. Watchful prayer is persistent. It is inclusive of everyone and of everything of which we know concerning the saints of God. It is staying at the work of prayer and not going to sleep spiritually on the needs of the times. It involves thinking on the issues and speaking to God about them for as long as it takes to get an answer.

THE REASON FOR IT ALL

The piece of the whole armor of God of prayer, as we have seen, is comforting and restful on one hand and combative and exhausting on the other hand. After speaking of prayer, Paul reminds us of the reason for all the concern about wearing the whole armor of God and walking consistently by faith. The reason is that we all might be boldly engaged in advancing the gospel among all nations of the earth. Forwarding obedience to the faith, getting the gospel, the good news of eternal salvation through Jesus Christ to all peoples is the urgent need and reason for it all. Advancing the gospel is an encroachment into enemy held territory. The enemy will not take this without a fight. Thus, the need for the ambassadors of Christ to have the protection of the whole armor of God.

Prayer is that final piece of the armor in one sense, and the piece which leads back into the whole cycle of the armor again and again. When we pray over the Word we have read and learned, another revolution of the protective cycle starts all over. God leads us into more truth, more understanding, more application, more consistency, more cleanness of heart, more strength to stand against the enemy, and more communion with himself. This way of life is what it means to walk in the Spirit. It is what it means to live according to the ways of the Lord. It is what it means to wear the whole armor of God.

CHAPTER 9

KEEPING IT RIGHT

*Put on the whole armour of God, that ye may be able to
stand against the wiles of the devil.
(Ephesians 6:11)*

The command to put on the whole armor of God is a
command which speaks of one-time action. We are not
told to put on the armor and take it off again. We are
not instructed to put on the armor in the same way that
we dress for each day's activities, and then take it off as
we remove our clothes in the evening before bedtime.
As a believer, we must come to a place in our life when
we make the decision to put on the whole armor of God
once and for all and to walk consistently by faith as God
requires of his followers.

It has been my observation that many believers who
do not understand the proper way to wear the armor
attempt to wear it in one of two ways. Some believers
have the "in case of emergency, break glass" mindset
concerning the armor. These are the Christians who do
not wear the armor as a lifestyle. They hope they can
grab it and symbolically put it on when they come into
a difficult experience in life. As we have already said,

this is not the way the armor is intended to be worn and trying to wear it this way does not work.

Another group of believers attempt to wear the armor not really knowing how it is to be worn and how it is to work. They appear much like David must have appeared and much like he must have felt when he put on the armor of King Saul before going out to fight Goliath. The armor did not fit. It was cumbersome. It was uncomfortable. It got in the way. It had not been tried by David. It could have spelled defeat for him had he worn it into battle with the giant. The experience of many Christians with the whole armor of God is that they tried it improperly, and it did not work for them. The truth is this: if you are not wearing the whole armor of God as a way of life, it is not going to work for you. It is when we wear the armor as a lifestyle that we can have its protection as a result of a consistent walk of faith.

A MEANS OF RE-CALIBRATION

Another wonderful thing about the whole armor of God lifestyle is that it serves as a means of re-calibrating our life when we get off track. The Bible says that if we will walk in the Spirit, we will never sin. This is another way to say wear the whole armor of God and you will walk consistently by faith. This is another example that the Bible itself is the best commentary on the Bible. Paul's letter to the Ephesians is the Biblical commentary on how to walk in the Spirit. To walk in the Spirit is to wear the whole armor of God. And to wear to whole armor of God is to walk by faith.

The problem with the followers of God is that we do not walk in the Spirit all of the time. At times, we give in to the flesh. We let the flesh have its way. We get caught off guard. We are ambushed by the enemy. We take a hit and never see it coming. We find ourselves in the same predicament as Paul in Romans seven: the good we want to do, we cannot do at times, and the evil we do not want to do is that which we end up doing. What can we do when this becomes our sad experience?

When we realize we have sinned, taken a misstep, or that something just is not right, we can go to the whole armor of God process and find exactly when and where we got off track. Perhaps things went wrong when we failed to expose our heart to the truth. Maybe we did not do the work to understand the truth God had shown us. Or we failed to apply the truth in our daily life. Maybe we have just been inconsistent in our faith walk. It could be that we have allowed ourself to think carnal, unclean thoughts. Perhaps we have given place to the devil and to demons in our life, failing to drive them out as Israel failed to do in Canaan, the land of promise. Maybe we have not spent time in the Word of God or in communing prayer with God. With the whole armor of God process, we can pinpoint the place where we failed to wear a certain piece or pieces of the armor, thus where the enemy was able to get a fiery dart through to our life. Take a look at the lists in Appendix 2. They show ways we can know when we are wearing the armor, and when we are not wearing it.

When we identify the place where the failure took place, we go back to that place and repair the breech in the protective wall. We repent of the sin, we pick ourself up, we dust ourself off, and we get up and continue the walk of faith once again. As we do this, the protection from the armor is there again and will be there until and unless we fail to walk in faith again.

God has provided a wonderful means of protecting the child of God who walks in the Spirit, who wears the whole armor of God. To wear the armor is a way of life. This statement is the key to the consistent walk of faith that we all desire to have and which is available to us simply by living our life in this way. As we close this short but powerful, life changing look at this way of life, let me challenge you to give this process a try. You will find that the process works and you can finally have a consistent walk of faith. Isn't this what you have always wanted as a believer in Christ? Why not put it into practice? See the whole armor of God work for you, producing a life of faith unto the pleasing of the Lord. Your service to God and the advancement of the gospel in our time depends upon it.

APPENDIX 1

Allen L. Elder

THE WHOLE ARMOR OF GOD

1) GT	7) P
2) BR	6) SS
3) SG	5) HS

— COMMENCE —

— CONTINUE —

4) SF

— CONSISTENCY —

FIGURE 1-1

75

Allen L. Elder

The Balanced Life

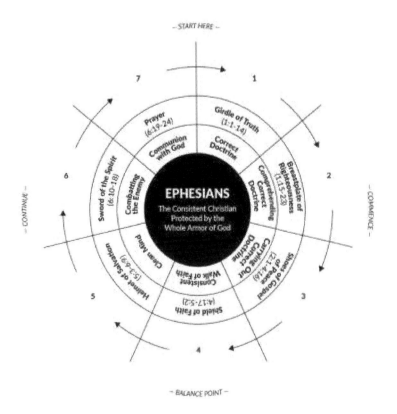

FIGURE 1-2

Allen L. Elder

APPENDIX 2

Allen L. Elder

Use these diagnostic sheets to tell when you are and when you are not wearing the whole armor of God. These lists are not exhaustive but exemplary.

THE GIRDLE OF TRUTH – CORRECT DOCTRINE
(Ephesians 1:1-14)

A. Ways to know you are wearing this piece of the whole armor of God.
1. Reading the Word of God
2. Seeing God's standards
3. Noting Scriptural connections
4. Close to God
5. Exposing myself to the Word of God
6. Seeking God in his Word
7. Seeking God's will in his Word
8. Cultivating devotional time with God
9. Hiding God's Word in my heart
10. Studying the Word of God
11. Spiritually strong
12. Stable
13. Grounded in the Bible
14. Sure of salvation
15. Exploring and adjusting to the deep doctrines of the Word of God

B. Ways to know you are not wearing this piece of the whole armor of God.
1. Not reading the Word of God
2. Leaning to my own understanding
3. Lost in the Word of God
4. Disconnected from God
5. No input from the Bible in my life
6. Opening self to wrong sources of counsel
7. Opposing God's will in my life
8. Lack of reverence toward God
9. Missing the benefits of the Word of God in my life

10. Not studying the Word of God
11. Spiritually weak
12. Unstable in some areas of my life
13. Loose footing – open to wrong beliefs
14. Wrestling with assurance of salvation
15. Content with shallow Bible study

THE BREASTPLATE OF RIGHTEOUSNESS – COMPREHENDING CORRECT DOCTRINE
(Ephesians 1:15-23)

A. Ways to know you are wearing this piece of the whole armor of God.
  1. Meditating on the Word of God
  2. Connecting the dots in the Word of God
  3. Experience spiritual awakenings
  4. Illumination of the Word by the Holy Spirit
  5. Gaining insight
  6. Experiencing spiritual discernment
  7. Formulating a plan for God's purpose in my life
  8. Learning, loving, and living God's will
  9. Knowing my value/worth to God
  10. Experiencing the power of God in my life
  11. Knowing I am part of the body of Christ
  12. Recognizing Jesus as head of the body of Christ

B. Ways to know you are not wearing this piece of the whole armor of God.
  1. Unconcern about the work of God's Word
  2. Stymied progress in spiritual growth
  3. In the dark spiritually
  4. Not experiencing the Holy Spirit with the Word of God
  5. Frustration with no progress
  6. Cannot make good decisions on a spiritual level
  7. Directionless

8. Dealing with insignificance
9. Dealing with insecurity
10. Dealing with insufficiency
11. Experiencing isolation and loneliness
12. Assuming authority or allowing usurped authority to others

THE SHOES OF THE PREPARATION OF THE GOSPEL OF PEACE – CARRYING OUT CORRECT DOCTRINE
(Ephesians 2:1-3:21)

A. Ways to know you are wearing this piece of the whole armor of God.
1. Trying to adapt to the Word of God
2. Applying the Word of God to my life
3. Obedience
4. Separating myself to God and from the world
5. Practicing personal sanctification
6. Being Christ's witness
7. Evangelizing
8. Making disciples
9. Aware of the times of the present age
10. Trusting God for big, impossible things
11. Making room for others
12. Walking in the light of God
13. Walking in step with the church
14. Cultivating an intentional and strategic global witnessing strategy

B. Ways to know you are not wearing this piece of the whole armor of God.
1. The Word of God has little effect in my life
2. Not living according to the Word of God
3. Disobedient to God
4. Lack of discipline in my life

5. Lack of self-control
6. Apathetic about representing Christ
7. Little to no evangelizing
8. Unconcern with the great commission
9. Biblically out of step with the age
10. Spiritually living on crumbs – playing it safe
11. Lacking in longsuffering toward others
12. Dabbling in darkness
13. Distant from the church
14. Living for right now and wishing to have a significant life

THE SHIELD OF FAITH – WALKING CONSISTENTLY WITH GOD BY FAITH
(Ephesians 4:1-5:2)

A. Ways to know you are wearing this piece of the whole armor of God.
1. Trusting God
2. Practicing the whole armor of God lifestyle
3. Growing consistently
4. Serving God and others
5. Consistent in most areas of my life
6. Walking in the Spirit
7. Giving place to God in my life
8. Controlling anger
9. Controlling the tongue
10. Sensitive to the Holy Spirit
11. Kind to others
12. Forgiving others
13. Developing and deploying myself in God's purpose
14. Practicing and promoting unity through doctrine and purpose
15. Walking in the new man (Spirit)

B. Ways to know you are not wearing this piece of the whole armor of God.
1. Eyes on my circumstances
2. Hit and miss with the armor of God
3. Stagnant in my relationship with God
4. Serving myself
5. Inconsistent in most areas of my life
6. Walking in the flesh
7. Giving place to the devil in my life
8. Controlled by anger
9. Uncontrolled speech
10. Grieving the Holy Spirit
11. Rude and unkind to others
12. Unforgiving
13. Living without purpose – insignificantly
14. Divided over beliefs
15. Walking in the old man (Flesh)

THE HELMET OF SALVATION – CLEAN MIND
(Ephesians 5:3 – 6:9)

A. Ways to know you are wearing this piece of the whole armor of God.
1. Focusing on God
2. Focusing on God's purpose
3. Controlling my thoughts
4. Resisting temptation
5. Worshipful heart
6. Faithful to God
7. Strong marriage relationship
8. Good relationship with my children in the home
9. Good relationships at work
10. Filled with the Spirit
11. Steadfast
12. Encouraging myself and others in the Lord
13. Thankful

14. Submissive

B. Ways to know you are not wearing this piece of the whole armor of God.
1. Taken my eyes off God
2. Focusing on the lust of the flesh, the lust of the eyes, and the pride of life
3. Letting my thoughts control me
4. Giving in to temptation – sinning
5. Cold or lukewarm toward God
6. Unfaithful to God
7. Struggling marriage relationship
8. Poor relationship with my children
9. Poor relationships at work
10. Spiritually depleted
11. Easily deceived
12. Discouraging attitude and words
13. Unthankful
14. Rebellious

THE SWORD OF THE SPIRIT – COMBATTING THE ENEMY
(Ephesians 6:10-18)

A. Ways to know you are wearing this piece of the whole armor of God.
1. Standing in the Lord's power
2. Wearing the whole armor of God as a lifestyle
3. Realizing the enemy is spiritual
4. Exercising the weapons of the warfare
5. Standing strong

B. Ways to know you are not wearing this piece of the whole armor of God.
1. Trying to stand in my own strength
2. I have let my guard down in one or more areas

3. Aiming the battle at people
4. Not using the weapons of the warfare
5. An easy target for the enemy

PRAYER – COMMUNION WITH GOD
(Ephesians 6:19-24)

A. Ways to know you are wearing this piece of the whole armor of God.
   1. Praying consistently
   2. Praying about everything
   3. Hearing from God in prayer
   4. Praying according to God's will
   5. Praying in conjunction with the Word of God
   6. Speaking to others about God
   7. Taking heed to my ministry
   8. Praying for others

B. Ways to know you are not wearing this piece of the whole armor of God.
   1. Inconsistent prayer life
   2. Praying sporadically about specific issues
   3. Not hearing from God in prayer
   4. Praying according to my will
   5. Praying apart from the Word of God
   6. Leaving God out of my conversations
   7. Careless about my ministry
   8. Forgetting others in prayer

Allen L. Elder

ABOUT THE AUTHOR

Allen L. Elder is an ordained pastor serving Southern Baptist Churches in his home state of South Carolina for nearly forty years. His ministry focus is upon personal disciple-making in fulfillment of the Lord's great commission, and the training of pastors in other countries. Allen is a husband, father, grandfather, and a Veteran of the United States Air Force. He is the founder of The LIFE Network.

Allen is interested in your response to his writings. You may contact him at allenelder@att.net.

Allen L. Elder

OTHER BOOKS BY THE AUTHOR

1. Building Disciples Requires Building Curriculum
   Author House

2. Ministering as a Deacon
   Cross Books

3. The LIFE Plan, Volume 1 – Genesis 1-11
   Amazon.com

4. The LIFE Plan, Volume 2 – Genesis 12 - Malachi
   Amazon.com

5. The LIFE Plan, Volume 3 – The Structure of the Bible
   Amazon.com

6. The LIFE Plan, Volume 4 – The Life of Christ on Earth
   Amazon.com

7. The LIFE Plan, Volume 5 – The Church
   Amazon.com

8. The LIFE Plan, Volume 6 – Your Part in the Story
   Amazon.com

   The Entire LIFE Plan is also available in Spanish
   from The LIFE Network.

9. The LIFE Network Pastor Training Plan – India
   Edition
   Available in English, Odiya, Hindi, and Telugu from
   The LIFE Network

Allen L. Elder

Made in the USA
Middletown, DE
22 August 2024

58985750R00057